I WANT TO BE A DATA SCIENTIST

Written by
Jonathan Reule

Illustration
Chong Wey Ming

First paperback edition May 2023
ISBN 978-981-18-6518-3

Published by Unibino Pte. Ltd.
31 Rochester Drive Level 3, #03-47 Singapore 138637

www.unibino.com

The type of work that data scientists do has been around for thousands of years, but the term 'data scientist' is relatively new. For ages, we have been recording patterns and trying to make such information meaningful. Being able to recognise patterns and make calculated decisions based on those observations has been important to our survival as a species.

For example, some early civilisations used to keep track of time by recording the cycles of the moon. This way, we could accurately predict the change in seasons and make plans based on these observations.

As villages expanded and became bigger cities, we used our record-keeping abilities to improve our way of life. Several governments in the past started keeping records of their crops' production and harvest so they could know if they had enough food for their people to survive the upcoming winter.

Ancient China also kept records of their citizens, especially the men of fighting age, in case they needed to go to war. With this information, they could form better strategies for upcoming battles and were able to better estimate their odds of victory.

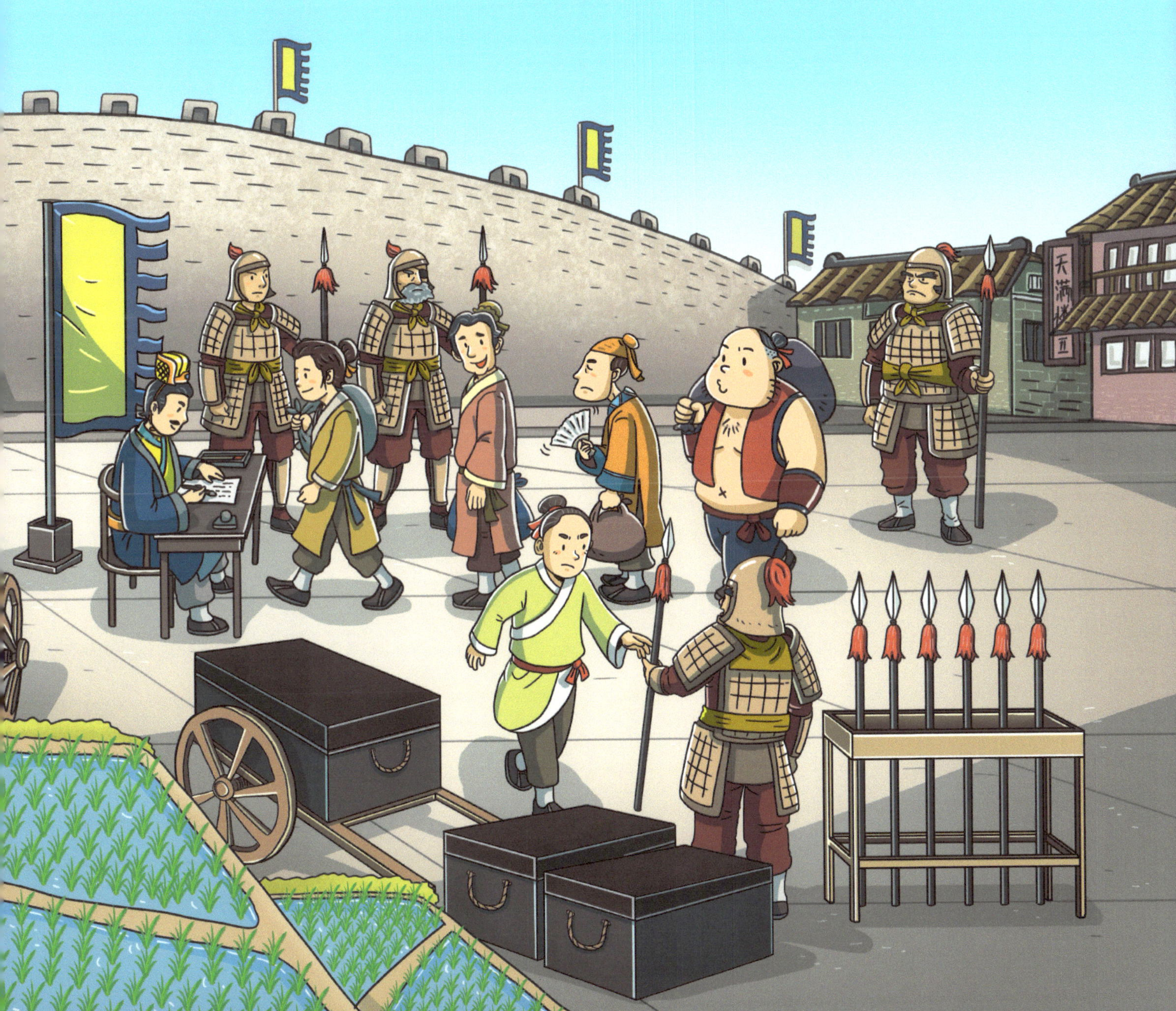

Recording data and statistics became more necessary as time passed. In mediaeval Europe, the Black Death spread to hundreds of millions of people, and many eventually died from the illness.

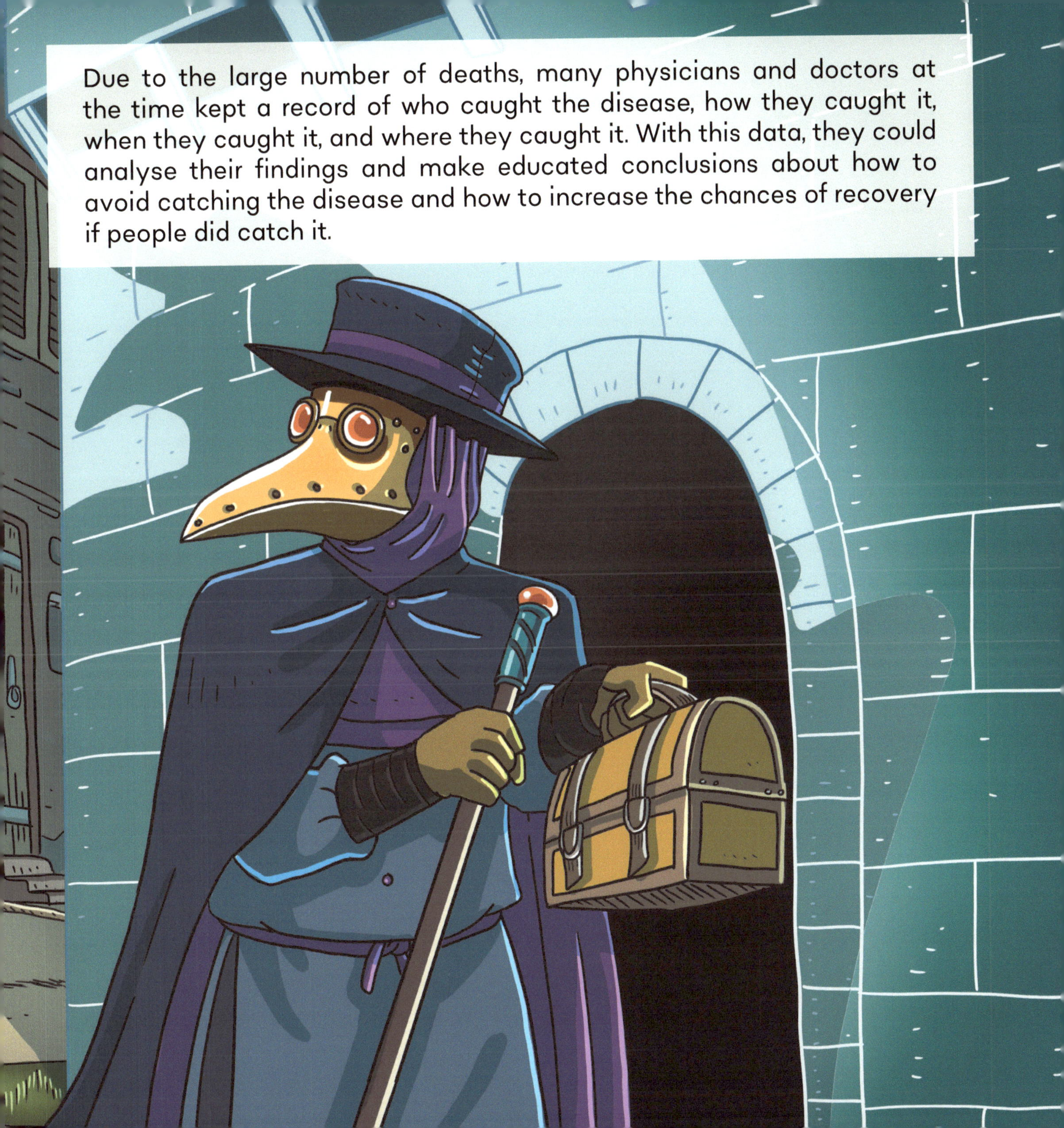

Due to the large number of deaths, many physicians and doctors at the time kept a record of who caught the disease, how they caught it, when they caught it, and where they caught it. With this data, they could analyse their findings and make educated conclusions about how to avoid catching the disease and how to increase the chances of recovery if people did catch it.

Throughout most of history, records were relatively obscure, given that they were handwritten or stored in private locations. Then the printing press was invented, which made sharing records easier and public libraries more common.

With the birth of the printing press, the amount of information that could be recorded and distributed grew exponentially. It now only took a few years to make a hundred copies of a single book rather than the several decades it took previously. As it became easier to publish and distribute text, newsprint was created, and people could get more frequent updates on what was happening around them.

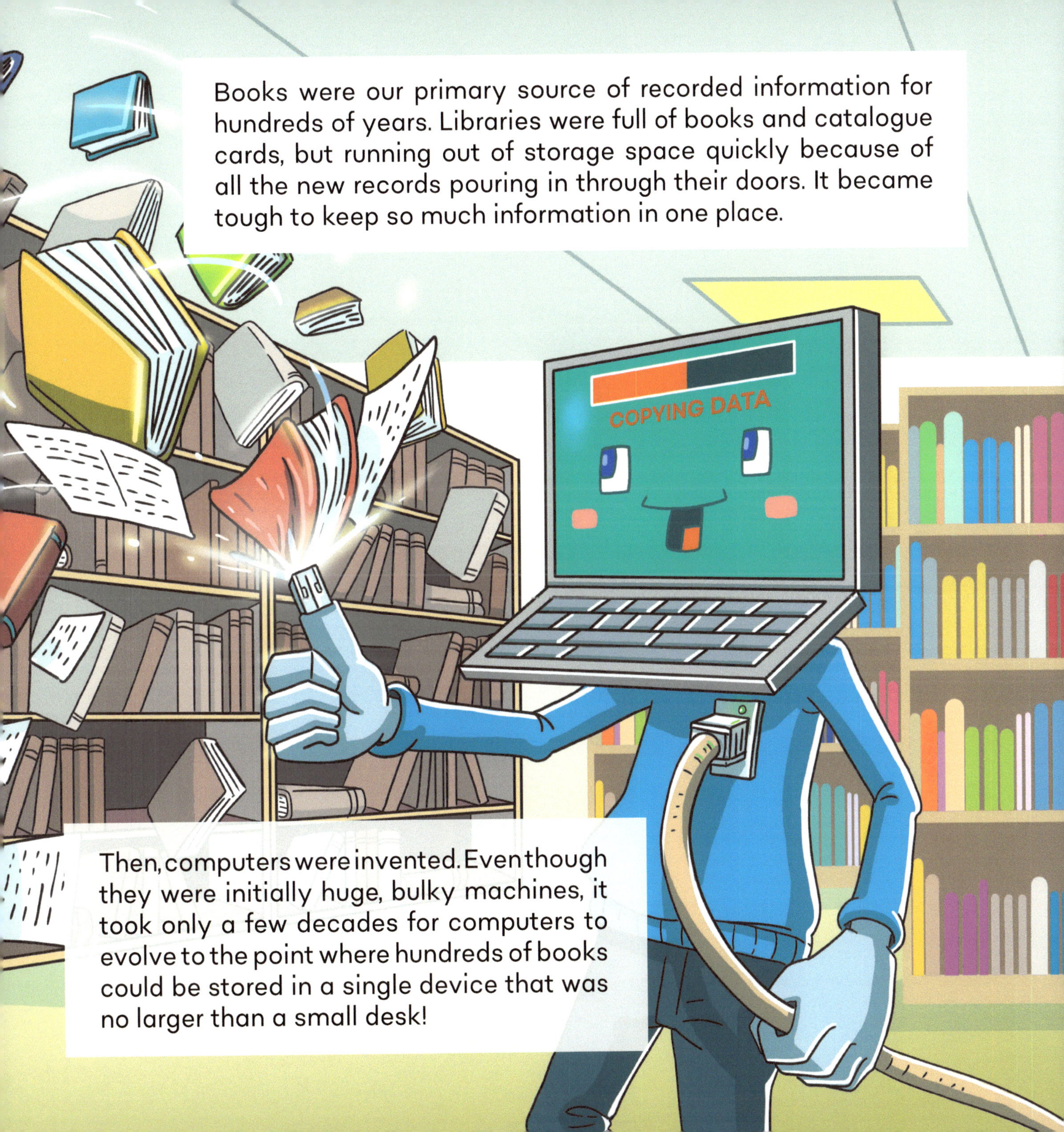

Books were our primary source of recorded information for hundreds of years. Libraries were full of books and catalogue cards, but running out of storage space quickly because of all the new records pouring in through their doors. It became tough to keep so much information in one place.

Then, computers were invented. Even though they were initially huge, bulky machines, it took only a few decades for computers to evolve to the point where hundreds of books could be stored in a single device that was no larger than a small desk!

Soon, it became clear that computers were great record keepers. They took up less physical space than books and offered large storage capacities, measured in bytes, so that we could fill our computers with heaps of information.

Computers also made it easier for us to share information like never before. After Tim Berners-Lee invented the Internet, we could send data and files across the world in just a few seconds. With regular postage mail, it would have taken us weeks just to send a small envelope across the world!

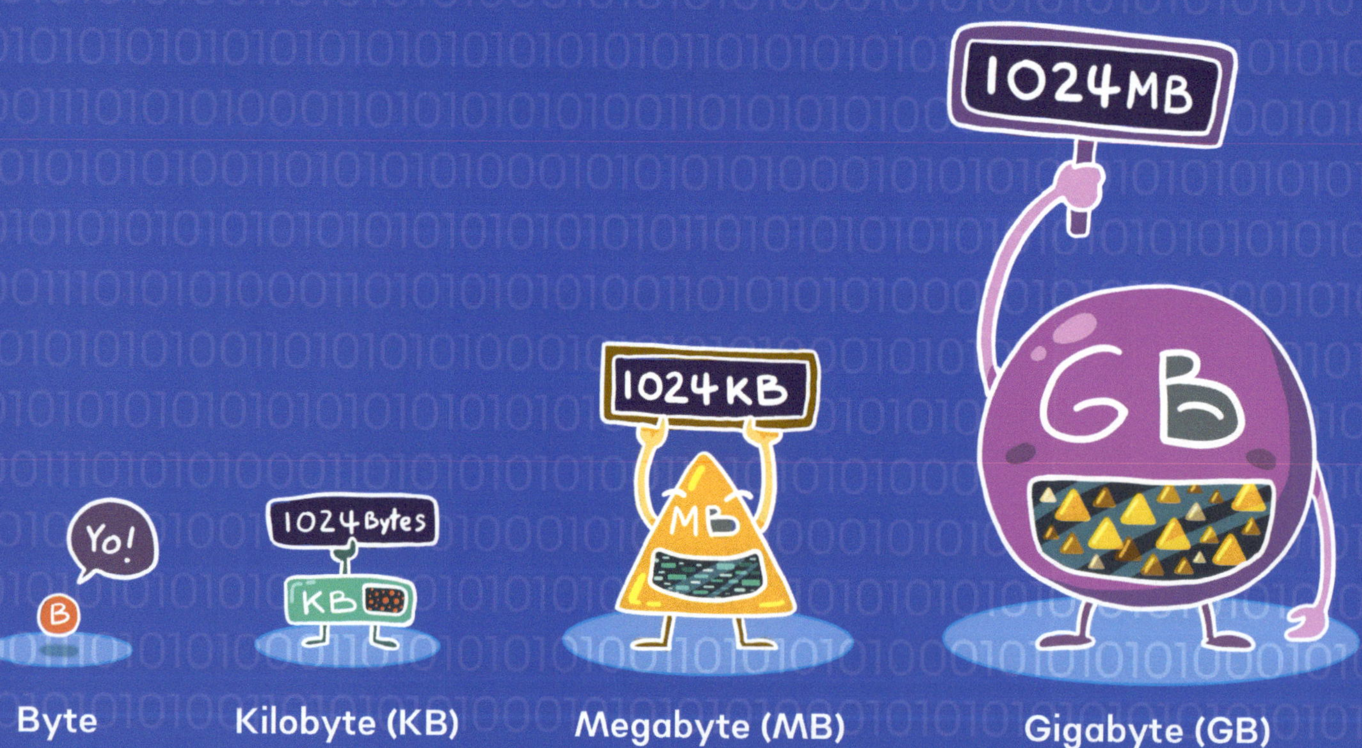

Byte

Kilobyte (KB)
1KB = 1024 Bytes

Megabyte (MB)
1MB = 1024 KB

Gigabyte (GB)
1GB = 1024 MB

Terabyte (TB)
1TB = 1024 GB

Petabyte (PB)
1PB = 1024 TB

These technological advances brought us to where we are today. With more and more people joining social media sites and using web applications, the amount of data that is being collected is ballooning out of control. We are no longer dealing with small, simple data sets but with petabytes of information.

On top of people creating data, there are now smart devices hooked up to the internet that are adding their own set of records too! For example, a smart bulb is a lightbulb that can change colours depending on the time of the day or even the type of movie you are watching, and much of that information gets stored as data.

This is why the role of data scientists is more important than ever. Data scientists are professionals who use their skills to analyse data sets and extract valuable insights from them. However, you have to be prepared to put in the time and practice to improve your skills.

Most data scientists will need to be able to write simple computer programmes and have a solid foundation in mathematics and logic, as these skills and knowledge will come in handy when analysing data. By using computer programmes and unique algorithms, they can sift through heaps of data and extract the necessary information they need quickly.

In the medical field, data scientists have been able to anticipate serious diseases in patients much earlier than before. By making use of data recorded by the patients' smart devices, such as watches or phones, and using their programming and mathematical skills, they can discover anomalies based on the patient's health history before these diseases become life-threatening.

There are also many data scientists hard at work to help with traffic control. If you have ever used a map application that helps you find the quickest route to take, you have interacted with the work of data scientists. By collecting traffic information and up-to-date road reports, data scientists can write computer programmes to crunch these numbers and determine how long it will take to reach your destination by reviewing all possible routes and calculating which one is the fastest!

Data scientists also play a key role in the field of artificial intelligence (AI) and machine learning. By creating computer systems that can learn and adapt to different situations to carry out specific operations. We have been able to accomplish some amazing feats, such as sending machines to dispose of deadly bombs and even sending spaceships and satellites to the moon!

BROOOMMM~
01
02
BEEP!
BEEP!
BEEP!
01:00

Data scientists also have a role in the financial industry. By analysing the data and information collected by the modern banking system, they have been able to efficiently help customers avoid risks and frauds that are happening more frequently these days.

Data scientists can be found working within the energy industry as well. By helping to determine how much energy is used and when the peak period is, they can determine to a high degree of accuracy how much energy is required to help run cities and towns. They also help with analysing the usage of renewable energy sources by determining their efficiency and finding areas of improvement.

You may not realise this, but data scientists are also needed within the travel industry. In the past, people would have to call airline and hotel companies in order to make a reservation. This made it difficult for customers to compare prices or know if they were getting the best deal available. Today, thanks to the algorithms developed by data scientists, it is really easy to look up dates that will give you the best prices for flights and hotels.

As you can see, many different industries hire data scientists. But if you wish to become one, you will need to take note of a few basic requirements first.

It is crucial to have a good grasp of the key fundamentals. Mathematics, statistics, and programming skills are vital in this field, so you will need to start working hard in these areas.
FORMULA
18
PROGRAMM
C++
PO3-C++
JAVA
- SPHERE -
Surface Area of
S=4πr²
-ALGEBRA FOR
a²-b²=(a-b
-FRACTIONS FORM
a/b×c/d=a
a²+2ab+b²
(b)²-2ab

The traditional path to becoming a data scientist is by obtaining a degree in computer science, mathematics or a related field. Getting a degree can give you an excellent foundation to start your journey, but this is not the only way.

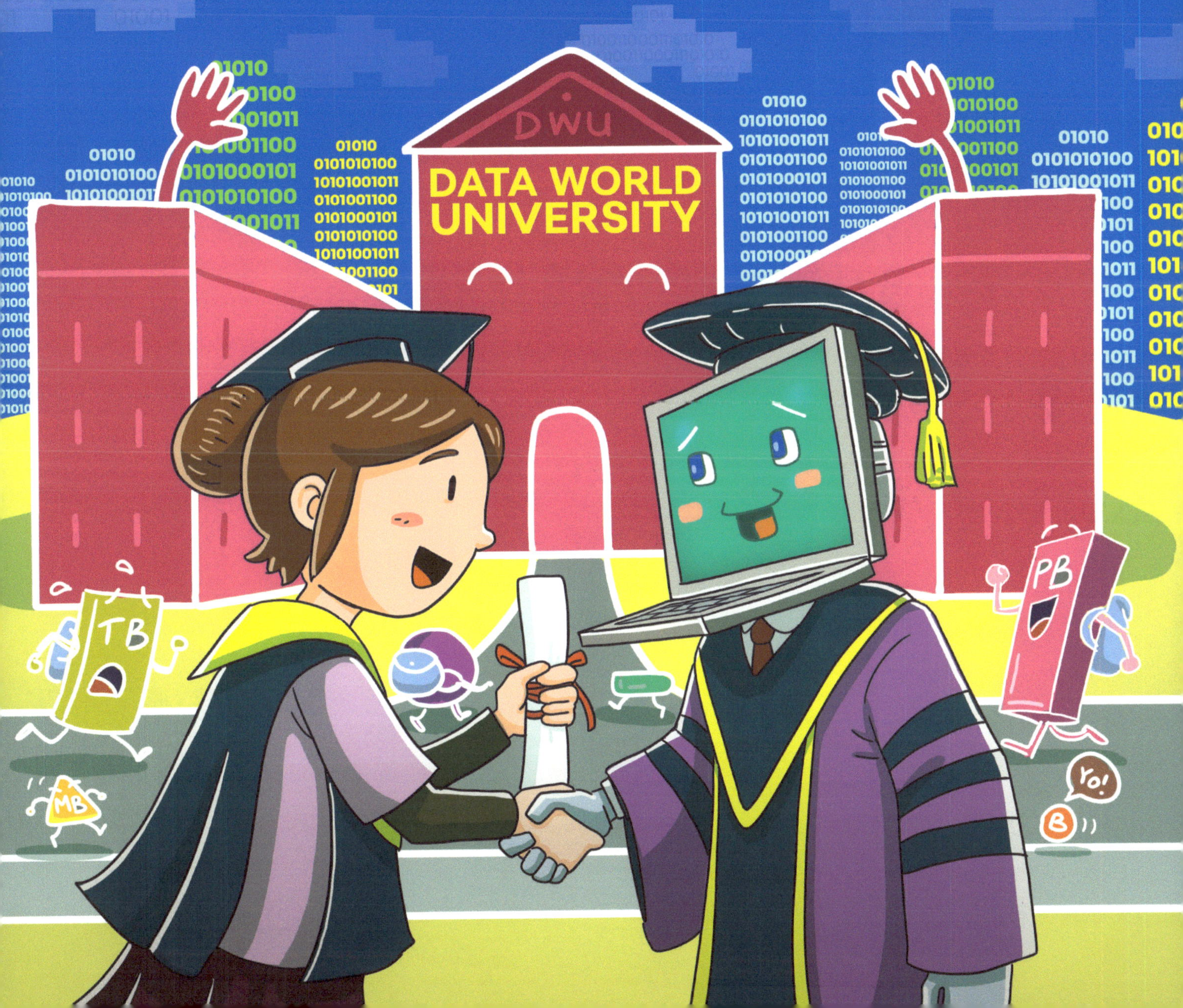

You can also attend a boot camp that specialises in data science, where you will be able to focus your learning on the key requirements. Many of these boot camps often run at night, which can be an excellent option for adults who are working in a different field and want to make a career switch.

There are also many data scientists who are self-taught, where they pick up the required skills by looking up resources such as tutorials and courses on the internet. As long as you have the dedication and discipline, you can achieve this at your own pace.

Next, you can think about which field of data science you are most interested in. Knowing your interests and passion can help you to focus your attention in the right direction and make your journey easier along the way.

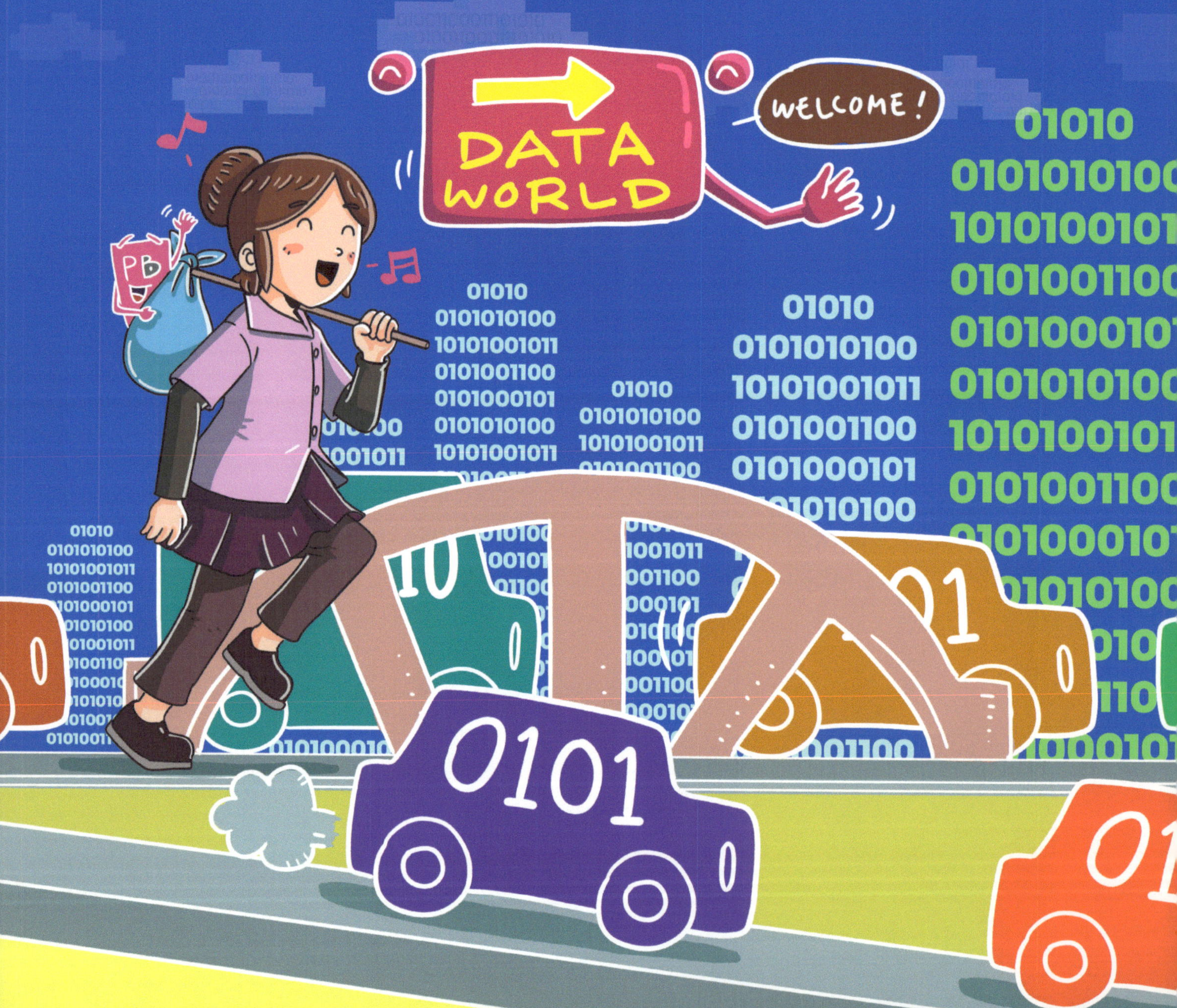

The tools used by data scientists are evolving together with the advancement of technology. You should keep up to date with the changes and developments in your field, as you will be able to learn new or better ways to perform your work more efficiently.

If you enjoy the challenge of making sense of numbers and large data sets, then you can consider being a data scientist.

As society keeps growing and expanding, our computers become more and more complex, and we will only have more data to process. Therefore, data scientists will always be needed in many different industries. The future is bright, and data scientists are here to stay.

Shubhi Saxena
Founder, Unibino

My Inspiration

As a parent in this ever-changing world, it can sometimes feel overwhelming when it comes to our children's futures. New technologies seem to be arising almost every day, and with so many innovations, it creates unique professions which many of us wouldn't have dreamed to be necessary only a few years ago. Which to me is a good thing. Because with so much variety, my children can have the opportunity to pick a career that will fit their personalities and build upon their strengths. As you may imagine, this desire within me to provide my children with the resources they needed to thrive, led me to search out books that would be easy enough for them to understand while teaching them about various professions.

Only, I found that these books were few and far between. Even if I could find a book about a certain profession geared towards young readers, I found them sparse inside and limited to only certain careers that may not fit my children's abilities. This is when I came up with the idea to write my own children's books, teaching them about all the various careers in the modern world. After months of researching different professions and learning more than I ever expected, I quickly realised this was going to be a bigger project than I first anticipated. I dove into the histories of these professions, discovering links to the past, and why these professions were now so important.

Ultimately my goal was to offer my children options, to show them that there is no one set path for everyone. But in this, I stumbled upon something bigger. I wanted to share this with future generations. To share with all children and parents about these careers, to help spark curiosity, and to instil a passion for the future. Everyone has special talents and abilities, and I hope that this series will be able to offer clarity and inspiration to children around the world. Because at the end of the day, it's never too early to start dreaming and never too late to take action. With this, I hope you enjoy this series and that your young ones become the best versions of themselves as they can achieve.

www.ingramcontent.com/pod-product-compliance
Ingram Content Group UK Ltd.
Pitfield, Milton Keynes, MK11 3LW, UK
UKHW060101300726
14090UKWH00003B/344

* 9 7 8 9 8 1 1 8 6 5 1 8 3 *